Meet

Spielberg

by Thomas Conklin

A Bullseye Biography

Random House  **New York**

For my mother

Photo credits: AP/Wide World Photos, p. 7, 15, 23, 34, 37, 39, 48, 51, 59, 60, 66, 74, 75, 79, 81; Retna Ltd.: A. D./All Action/Retna, 105, 107; Granitz/Retna, 10, 85; Harvey/Stills/Retna, 99; Holland/Retna, 50; McBride/Retna, 80; P. S./All Action/Retna, 104; Storm/Stills/Retna, 4; Star File: Shaw/Star File, 103 (right); Zuffante/Star File, 22, 67, 72, 103 (left), 109

A BULLSEYE BOOK PUBLISHED BY RANDOM HOUSE, INC.

Cover design by Fabia Wargin Design and Creative Media Applications, Inc.
Copyright © 1994 by Thomas Conklin
Published in the United States by Random House, Inc., New York, and simultaneously in Canada by Random House of Canada Limited, Toronto.

Library of Congress Cataloging-in-Publication Data
Conklin, Thomas
Meet Steven Spielberg / by Thomas Conklin.
   p.   cm. — (A Bullseye biography)
Summary: Examines the life and career of the successful film director, known for such popular movies as "Jaws," "Close Encounters of the Third Kind," and "E.T."
ISBN 0-679-85445-2 (trade)
1. Spielberg, Steven, 1947–   —Juvenile literature. 2. Motion picture producers and directors—United States—Biography—Juvenile literature. [1. Spielberg, Steven, 1947–
2. Motion picture producers and directors.] I. Title. II. Series.
PN1998.3.S65C66 1994
791.43'0233'092—dc20   93-4315

Manufactured in the United States of America   10 9 8 7 6 5 4 3 2 1

Contents

1

The Greatest Show on Earth

It is 1952. A man stands in the lobby of a movie theater, holding the hand of his five-year-old son, Steven. The man is preparing his son for a big event. The boy is about to see his very first movie.

"It's going to be bigger than you," the boy's father gently says. "But that's all right. The people in it are going to be up on a screen. They can't get out at you." And with that, the man leads Steven into the dark theater. They settle down to watch the movie, *The Greatest Show on Earth*.

The movie begins. It is about a circus. Steven sits in his seat, enchanted. The movie shows colorful, funny clowns. It's full of death-defying stunts, exciting chases, exotic and dangerous animals. And running the entire show is the circus boss—a handsome, tough, but kind man. He wears a leather jacket and a broad-brimmed hat, and keeps order by cracking a bullwhip.

As the movie goes on, Steven gets deeper and deeper into the story. Then, suddenly, something spectacular happens!

"There they were, up on that screen," Steven later remembered. "*And they were getting out at me.*" In other words, Steven's father had been wrong. The people on the screen no longer seemed "make-believe" to Steven. For the rest of the time he sat in the theater, Steven entered the world on the screen. It was a world of excitement, danger, comedy, and magic.

The boy was Steven Spielberg. He would

*Steven Spielberg where he likes to be most—
behind the camera.*

grow up to be one of the most successful moviemakers of all time. His work includes *Jurassic Park, Hook,* the Indiana Jones movies, and—the most popular movie ever made—*E.T. The Extra-Terrestrial.*

What is the key to Steven Spielberg's success? He has great talent. He works hard. (Sometimes he works twenty-four hours a day!) But perhaps the real key to Steven's success is that he remembers who his audience is. Steven never forgets that he is making his movies for a kid sitting in a dark theater—a kid filled with excitement, waiting for the magic to begin.

2

Scary Stories

Steven Spielberg was born on December 18, 1947, in Cincinnati, Ohio. His father, Arnold Spielberg, was an electrical engineer, and, later, a computer specialist. His mother, Leah, had been a concert pianist. When Steven grew up, he would combine his father's skill with mechanical things and his mother's talent as an artist.

Arnold Spielberg was a successful man. He frequently changed jobs, moving from one big company to another. This meant that the Spielbergs moved often as Steven was growing up. They went from Ohio to Had-

Father and son together in Los Angeles in 1988.

donfield, New Jersey, when Steven was still a young boy. They then moved to Phoenix, Arizona, where Steven lived until he was sixteen.

Steven had three younger sisters. They helped to keep him company as the family moved from place to place. They would also help Steven as he developed his talent—first as his audience, and then as actors in his early films.

When Steven was a small boy, it seemed unlikely that he would grow up to make movies. His parents carefully controlled everything Steven and his sisters watched on TV or in the movies. The Spielbergs tried to shelter their children from violence and bad language. They let the kids see only shows like Disney cartoons and family movies like *The Greatest Show on Earth*. At home, there was a blanket draped over the Spielbergs' TV set. It came off only for shows that Steven's parents thought were good for kids.

Because he was not allowed to watch often, Steven grew more and more interested in movies and television. His parents had helped him to realize how influential they could be. "I feel that perhaps one of the reasons I make movies all the time is because I was told not to," Steven later said.

The movies that he did see made a big impression on young Steven. While his parents saw the Disney cartoons as harmless fun, Steven saw the power in the stories they told. He was especially scared by the witches, sorcerers, and demons in the Disney movies. "Between *Snow White*, *Fantasia*, and *Bambi*, I was a basket case," Steven remembers.

Steven became a good storyteller. He first used his talent to frighten his three younger sisters. "I used to tell them bedtime horror stories all the time. I would make them up as I went along," Steven recalls. "I could feel my sisters twisting under the sheets and wanting to escape the room, and I'd make the stories more horrible." Afterward, Steven would often leave his sisters and go into the yard outside their bedroom. Then he would shine a flashlight through the window and scare the daylights out of the girls.

Steven also used "special effects" on his sisters. Once he saw a science fiction movie called *Invaders from Mars*. It was about aliens who tried to take over the Earth. The leader of the aliens was a huge head without a body, only long octopus arms coming out of its neck. The movie inspired Steven. He took a model skull, put a baseball cap on it, and shoved some red lights under the cap. He put the shining skull in a closet. Steven then blindfolded his sisters, put them in the closet with the skull, and locked the door. "They were screaming for hours," Steven later recalled.

Fortunately for Steven (and his sisters!), he soon found another outlet for his story-telling. By the time Steven was twelve years old, the family was living in the suburbs of Phoenix, Arizona. There, Steven played Little League baseball and was active in the Boy Scouts. He wanted to get his photography badge as a scout. So he went to his father and asked to borrow a camera.

Like many people in the 1950s, Arnold

Spielberg owned a small 8-millimeter camera for making home movies. (The millimeter measurement refers to the size of the film the camera uses. Most movies shown in theaters are on 70-millimeter film.) Arnold loaned the camera to Steven for his scout project. And from that moment on, Steven was hooked.

First, Steven set up a train wreck using model trains and filmed it. It was fun to watch, but it didn't really say much. For his next film, he decided to tell a story. He asked some of his friends to act in it. They got together and made a three-and-a-half-minute movie. It told a simple story—one of Steven's friends pretended to hold up a stagecoach; then he sat and counted the money.

Soon Steven was in charge of filming the family's events. He would record the action during outings and vacations. He learned how to set up shots. Instead of just pointing the camera and letting it run, he would figure out the best spot to shoot a scene from.

Steven sets up a shot for his blockbuster film
Close Encounters of the Third Kind.

Steven also taught himself to use different camera angles to make the shots look better. He learned tricks to create special effects that would fool the viewer.

Most important, Steven learned how to tell stories using a camera. It wasn't surprising that his first movies were horror stories.

Steven even let his sisters star in the stories. By the age of thirteen, Steven had received his first award for moviemaking. He won a local contest for a forty-minute war picture called *Escape to Nowhere*. Steven had received his first award for moviemaking!

Despite his growing skill, Steven Spielberg was an awkward boy. He was "the weird, skinny kid with acne," he remembers. Steven didn't have many friends. Nor was he a very good student. Although he was very bright, he never did terribly well in the classroom. But making movies gave him a way to express himself.

By the time he was in high school, Steven was devoting most of his time to making movies. Filmmaking is an expensive hobby, however. So Steven started his own landscaping business. He took the money he earned and used it to buy film and other moviemaking equipment.

Steven did find time for other interests.

Together with his dad, he spent many hours staring at the night sky, looking at the stars. The two of them shared a great interest in astronomy and science fiction. They wondered if there was life on other planets. Steven and his dad often talked about the possibility of UFOs bringing visitors from another planet. This interest in UFOs inspired Steven.

At the age of sixteen, Steven wrote his first full-length movie script. He called it *Firelight*. The story was about scientists studying a group of strange lights in the skies. The strange lights turned out to be spaceships. They landed on Earth, bringing terrible creatures that, in Steven's words, "gobbled up everything in sight."

Steven's dad admired his son's work, and so he gave Steven the $500 he needed to make the movie. By the time *Firelight* was done, Steven had made a two-and-a-half-hour "8-millimeter epic." The Spielberg family asked the local movie theater to show the movie for one night. The theater managers agreed.

Today, Steven claims that *Firelight* is probably the worst movie ever made. But the people in his hometown did not think so. Many people came to see it. And even though it played for only one night in the theater, *Firelight* earned more than the $500 it had cost to make.

Steven Spielberg was on his way to becoming a professional moviemaker.

3

Amblin'

"My childhood was the most fruitful part of my entire life," Steven Spielberg once said. Growing up in the suburbs gave Steven many memories of everyday life in America. He often uses those memories when he plans his movies. "I go back there to find ideas and stories," he says.

But before he could become a movie-maker, Steven needed more experience. Simply making films with a home-movie camera was not enough. He needed to learn more about the technical aspects of making movies. And most moviemakers learn their trade at film school.

Why do some people go to school to learn moviemaking, just as other people study to be doctors or lawyers? Filmmaking is a very difficult business. A movie director needs to have many different skills. And film school is the best place to learn those skills.

First, a director needs to have a good "eye." Like a painter, a movie director must be able to create an interesting picture. Every movie, television show, or video that you watch is made up of thousands of separate images, or pictures. A good director makes those pictures unforgettable.

Second, a director must be a good manager. Shooting a movie is a long and complicated business. Hundreds of different people work on a movie, each doing a different job. The director is in charge of them all. Without someone to keep things running smoothly, a movie can grow out of control. That can lead to disaster on a movie set.

Finally, and perhaps most important, a director must be a good storyteller. Different types of storytellers use different methods to tell a story. Novelists write down stories. Playwrights use actors and stage settings to tell their stories. A movie director must use all of these things—and more. A script, actors, lighting, music, and special effects all come together in a movie. A director must be able to combine all of these things to tell a good story.

Most film schools are part of bigger colleges. Many of the best are in Los Angeles, home of Hollywood and the center of the moviemaking industry. By the time Steven was ready to leave high school, his family had moved to California. It seemed likely that Steven would go to one of L.A.'s top film schools. Perhaps he would study at the

*Steven with his good friend and
colleague George Lucas.*

University of Southern California (USC). The
USC film school had star students like
George Lucas, who would go on to make the
Star Wars movies.

But there was one major problem. Steven
had spent most of his time in high school
making movies. By the time he left high

school, he had made dozens of movies. But he hadn't spent much time studying. His grades were low. So low, in fact, that he couldn't get into any of the best film schools.

Steven was not discouraged, though. He enrolled in a good but less famous college, California State College at Long Beach. Steven studied English in college. And he

Steven and George goofing around outside of Mann's Chinese Theater.

continued to teach himself the art of film-making. But he knew he still needed to learn more.

In order to get a firsthand education, Steven came up with a way to watch moviemakers at work at one of Hollywood's biggest studios—Universal Studios.

Today, Universal and other movie studios have created theme parks on their lots. They have rides, shows, and other attractions. Visitors are welcome to come in and see behind the scenes of moviemaking. But back in the 1960s and 1970s, a studio was a place where movies were made—nothing more. It was nearly impossible for a visitor to get past the doors of a studio. Still, Steven knew that was the best place to continue his education.

To get on the sets, Steven knew he would have to give up his usual blue jeans and T-shirt. So he put on a suit and tie and carried a briefcase. And although he was just a college kid hoping to break into movies,

Steven walked right up to the Universal Studios gates. He seemed so sure of himself that the guards let him through. Steven snuck into the studio so often he found an empty office in one of the buildings and claimed it as his own!

Once he was inside, Steven would head to sets where movies were being made. This gave him a great opportunity. He was able to watch some of the best directors as they worked. For instance, Alfred Hitchcock filmed at Universal Studios. Hitchcock had made dozens of thrilling movies, including *The Birds* and *North by Northwest*. Steven sneaked onto the set of Hitchcock's spy thriller *Torn Curtain,* starring Paul Newman and Julie Andrews. He watched how Hitchcock set up his shots. And he was able to see how a master like Hitchcock handled a large cast of actors and a crew of workers.

Steven also continued to make his own movies. At this stage of his life, he was doing a lot of experimenting. Steven's movies were very personal. He was not trying to entertain large audiences. He was trying out new styles and story ideas.

Steven showed those movies to Hollywood producers, hoping they would hire him. But no one was interested. If he wanted to make a living making movies, Steven would have to find a way to prove that he could do the job. So he decided to make something that would show the producers that he could handle a camera and a cast.

The result was a movie called *Amblin'*. It was a romantic story about a boy and a girl who hitchhike across the Mojave Desert to the Pacific Ocean.

Making a romance was quite a change for a kid who had grown up on horror and science fiction. Steven himself does not think much of the movie now. He has called *Amblin'* "the slick by-product of a kid immersed up to his nose in film."

But slick or not, the movie did what Steven hoped it would do. *Amblin'* won awards at film festivals in Venice, Italy, and Atlanta, Georgia. Universal Pictures bought the rights to the movie and marketed it as a double feature with *Love Story*. A tear-jerking romance based on a best-selling novel, *Love Story* was a huge hit in 1970. As a result, millions of people saw Steven's first movie.

Steven's career was off to an impressive start. At age thirteen, he had won his first award for filmmaking. At age sixteen, he had shown his first movie at his hometown theater. And at age twenty, he had a movie playing in theaters all across the country! *Amblin'* opened the door for Steven. Today his production company, Amblin Entertainment, is named after his first hit.

In 1970, Steven Spielberg left college. He returned to Universal Studios in Hollywood. But this time, he didn't have to sneak onto the lot. Steven Spielberg had signed a contract to make TV shows for Universal.

Young, smart, and talented, Steven had taught himself how to make movies. And now he was ready to show the world what he could do.

4
Getting Control

Steven's first job was to direct an episode of a horror series called *Night Gallery*. It was created by Rod Serling, the man who made *The Twilight Zone*—one of Steven's favorite TV shows when he was growing up.

The *Night Gallery* episode Steven directed was about an old blind woman. The woman was very rich, but she was also very mean. Everyone who knew her hated her. The woman's doctor told her of a new kind of operation—transplanting. If she got new eyes, there was a chance she might get her vision back, the doctor said. Desperate to see, the woman bought eyeballs from a poor man. At midnight on a dark night, the doctor transplanted the eyeballs. He then left the woman, telling her to take off the bandages in a few hours. Alone in her luxurious penthouse, the woman removed the bandages, but she still couldn't see. Frantic, thinking that she was still blind, the woman jumped out of a window to her death.

What the old woman didn't know was that just as she took off the bandages, there was a power blackout. All she had to do was wait for the sun to rise!

The story was very spooky, and Steven did a great job directing it. The old lady was played by Joan Crawford. She had been one of the biggest stars in Hollywood for more than fifty years. She was known to be very hard to work with. But at the age of twenty-one, Steven handled her like a pro. "It was extraordinary," said one man who worked on the show. "This kid was in complete control of a star like Crawford."

After *Night Gallery,* Steven was hired to direct a number of TV shows. The episodes he made were often much better than the regular shows. But Steven wasn't happy working in TV. He didn't feel he had enough control over his work. Even a talented director has little control when directing for television. Final decisions are made by network executives—such as the people who run NBC, ABC, or CBS. And the directors have to listen to what the executives say.

"When I was a young director in TV, I had no real pull. The network people would come in and say, 'I don't like that. Do it over again,'" Steven remembers. Steven didn't like having other people tell him what to do. "It was real tough for me," he said. "That's why I didn't do television very long."

Fortunately, Steven was so talented that his skills came through even on TV. In 1971, he was hired to direct a TV movie called

Duel. It was a simple story. A man driving a car in the desert is chased by a huge diesel truck. The man has no idea why the truck is after him, but it keeps trying to run him over. For an hour and a half, the truck stalks the man. The tension builds and builds—until finally the man "outduels" the killer truck.

Told like this, the story doesn't seem that scary. But in Steven Spielberg's hands, it became a terrifying movie. It was a huge hit on TV. It was shown in movie theaters in Europe and Japan. It earned more than $5 million and won many awards. To this day, many people still consider *Duel* the best movie ever made for television.

With the success of *Duel*, Steven became one of the hottest directors in Hollywood. Dozens of scripts were sent to him for his consideration. But he rejected them all. He had had enough of working on other people's stories. For his next projects, Steven wanted to work on his own stories.

5

A Monster of a Movie

In 1969, Steven clipped a newspaper article. It told of a woman who had kidnapped her baby from its foster parents. The woman had led police on a cross-country chase before she was finally caught. Steven decided that this true story would be the subject of his first major movie.

Steven called the movie *The Sugarland Express*. Like *Duel*, it featured car chases galore. Only this time, instead of one truck chasing one car, Steven directed chases involving *200* cars! When it was released in

*Steven directs William Atherton and Goldie Hawn
in a scene from* The Sugarland Express.

1974, *The Sugarland Express* got strong reviews. Critics marveled at the way Steven handled the action. They also said that he really understood the people in his movie. They were typical, everyday people, caught up in things beyond their control.

That pretty much describes what would happen to Steven himself on his next movie.

While he was working on *The Sugarland Express,* Steven visited the movie company's offices. There he saw an advance copy of a new book called *Jaws*. It was about a monster shark that terrorizes a beach resort. Steven read the book and thought it would make a great movie. The producers agreed. In fact, they already had paid the book's author, Peter Benchley, $175,000 for the right to make the movie!

But who would direct *Jaws*? The producers had paid a lot of money for the rights. Making the movie would take a lot of skill. It would call for crowd scenes, scenes shot on boats, and numerous underwater scenes. It made sense to hire a veteran director to make the movie. But there was one director who wanted the challenge more than anyone else—Steven Spielberg.

"I wanted to do *Jaws* for hostile reasons," Steven later said. "I read it and felt that *I* had been attacked. It terrified me, and I wanted to strike back." Steven got his wish. The producers had been impressed by *Duel*. They had seen how Steven had managed to make a simple diesel truck seem like a terrifying monster. They also knew that he could handle a large production like *The Sugarland Express*. So, at the age of twenty-six, Steven Spielberg was hired to film *Jaws*.

Steven and the producers decided to make the movie in a real town on the ocean. They also chose to shoot the underwater scenes in the ocean. "I could have shot the movie in a tank," Steven said, referring to the huge fish-tank-like structures that are often used to shoot underwater scenes. "But it would not have looked the same." Steven was very concerned that the movie look as authentic as possible.

The movie was set on Martha's Vineyard, a resort island off the coast of Massachusetts. Steven and his cast and crew went there in May of 1974. They expected to be

*A 26-year-old Steven on location
for the filming of* Jaws.

finished ten weeks later. They were wrong.

Everything that could go wrong did. First, there were problems with the local people.

Steven could handle the actors he had hired to be in the movie. But the people on Martha's Vineyard were a different story. Many people vacation on the island. They didn't like being told to stay off the beach while the movie was being made.

There was also a problem with sailboats. The climax of *Jaws* has the three heroes of the movie alone on a boat, battling the killer shark to the death. When the producers had first visited Martha's Vineyard, it was winter. The ocean was empty. It looked stark and menacing. It seemed as though it would be the perfect setting for the dramatic final scenes.

But in summer Martha's Vineyard is a very different place. Hundreds of sailboats fill the water. The atmosphere is very relaxed and happy. It's a great place to take a vacation—but not to film a scary movie. "You have three guys out in a rickety boat, hunting a killer shark," Steven later complained.

Steven in a lighthearted moment with Jaws *stars Roy Scheider and Richard Dreyfuss.*

"What kind of menace is there going to be if there is a family of four only fifty feet away, having a picnic on their sailboat?"

Despite all these problems, Steven managed to get the movie under control. But it took much longer than anyone expected. The ten weeks that the shooting was scheduled to take came and went. And still the movie was long from finished.

New problems came up with sharks. It wasn't that the crew was bothered by sharks in the water. The problem was, they couldn't find any nearby!

One scene in the movie calls for local fishermen to catch a huge shark. Everyone on the island mistakenly believes it is the killer. Thinking that it is safe, the people head back to the beach—and back to the real killer shark! It is a very important twist in the story. In order to get the full effect from the scene, Steven insisted on using a real shark to "play" the dead shark. So he hired local fishermen to catch one. They kept bringing in sharks—and Steven kept rejecting them. They were all too small. Finally, Steven sent away to Florida for a dead shark. At thirteen feet long, it would be big enough for the part.

The shark was put on ice and sent to

Massachusetts. But by the time it got there, the dead shark was pretty smelly. After four days of shooting, the smell was almost unbearable. The local people were outraged. To show how they felt, they put their *own* dead sharks at the doorstep of the producer's cottage.

It was starting to seem that things couldn't get any worse. Then the real star of the movie showed up.

To portray the killer shark, Steven hired special-effects artists to make mechanical models. They didn't make just one, though. They had to create three, each for different types of movements.

The model sharks were nicknamed "Bruce." Each "Bruce" was truly larger than life. Each was twenty-four feet long, weighed one and a half tons, and cost $150,000 to make. But even at that price, the models seemed doomed to go haywire.

The Bruce used for underwater scenes

was the most complex one of all. He was attached to a twelve-ton control panel that rested on the ocean floor. It took thirteen technicians in scuba gear to run him. Before he began filming the shark, Steven wanted to give him a few test swims. He had the technicians set him up. At last, everything was in place. Steven was ready to give Bruce his test swim. "Action!" the director yelled. Bruce shuddered, moved, began to swim...and then sank to the bottom of the ocean.

This was a big setback, but Steven refused to give up. He had the experts fix up Bruce. They prepared him for another test run. This time Bruce didn't sink. Instead, his motor exploded! They had to haul the model, all three thousand pounds of it, completely out of the water. They put it in dry dock and tried to fix the motor.

By this time, *Jaws* was far behind schedule. It was also costing much more money to make than anyone had expected. There were rumors that Steven was going to be fired. It wasn't his fault that things were not going smoothly, though. The movie itself was a huge challenge. "*Jaws* should never have been made," Steven later said. "It was an impossible effort."

Steven was exaggerating. *Jaws* was not impossible. But by the time it was done, the movie had taken twice as long and cost twice as much as anyone had expected. This put a lot of pressure on its young director. What if the movie was a flop? The studio had spent millions on it. If *Jaws* failed, Steven Spielberg's reputation as a good director would be ruined.

Jaws was scheduled to open in June 1975. Before a movie opens, the producers often show it to a preview audience. That way they know if they have a hit movie—or if it still needs work. Steven remembers the first preview of *Jaws*. "I was in a daze and couldn't sit down," Steven said. "I stood by the exit."

Steven observed the audience as they watched the movie. He couldn't tell if they liked it or not. Then, right after the shark kills its second victim, Steven saw a man get up from his seat. Steven watched, stunned, as the man headed for the door. The man began to trot—then run right past Steven and out the door. Steven thought to himself, "This guy not only hates the movie, he's *running* out of this film!"

But the man wasn't running out. Steven followed him. He watched as the man made it to the lobby, threw up—then rushed *back* into the theater! Even after being sick, the man couldn't wait to see the end of the movie. At that point, Steven breathed a sigh of relief.

So did the producers. *Jaws* was more than a success. It was a monster hit. It earned more than $60 million in one month—an all-time record. Critics raved about the movie. It was both a crowd pleaser and a well-made film. And Steven's attention to detail paid off. Even Bruce the shark was praised. "I was surprised how genuine he seemed," said Peter Gimbel, a filmmaker who made a documentary about great white sharks.

Steven was thrilled. He knew that he had pulled off a nearly impossible job. And best of all, he had pleased the toughest critics around—kids. "I really do think kids notice flaws in films more than adults," Steven says. "I get a lot of letters from kids who say, 'I love *Jaws* even though the shark was only mechanical.'"

With such a huge success under his belt, you would think that Steven would take the time to relax. But he didn't. Always a hard worker, Steven had been writing his next script while making *Jaws*.

In *Jaws*, Steven scared people with a monster from the ocean's depths. With his next movie, he wanted to awe them with visitors from outer space.

6

Close Encounters

The first movie that Steven Spielberg ever made, *Firelight*, had been about visitors from outer space. But that wouldn't be his last word on the subject. Not by a long shot.

Steven liked to read reports of UFOs. And he noticed something about all of the reports. While most movies about UFOs (including *Firelight*) showed aliens as evil creatures out to kill humans, the stories he read about "real" UFOs were very different. "In thirty years of UFO reportings, the encounters have been very friendly," Steven told a reporter. So he decided that his next movie would be about friendly aliens.

The movie was called *Close Encounters of the Third Kind*. "Close encounters" are meetings between humans and aliens from outer space. Close encounters of the first kind are when a person sees a UFO close up. A close encounter of the second kind is when someone sees a UFO close up—and it leaves physical evidence behind. In a close encounter of the third kind, a person sees both a UFO *and* its "occupants"....

Close Encounters of the Third Kind tells the story of normal, everyday people who see UFOs. At the end of the movie, a giant UFO lands on a mountain in Wyoming. It welcomes human beings aboard—and takes them off to the mysteries of outer space.

In many ways, *Close Encounters* was a more difficult movie to make than *Jaws*. It, too, was very expensive. So expensive that the studio making it could have gone out of business had the movie bombed. ("This will

Steven directs a huge crowd scene for Close Encounters.

be the best movie Steven ever made, or it will be the last," said a friend of his.)

Steven traveled all over the world to make *Close Encounters*. For one scene, he went to India. There he filmed 2,000 local people standing in rows and chanting. The scene went smoothly—until a jackrabbit ran through the crowd. "All two thousand people took off after the rabbit," Steven

48

remembered. "We didn't get them back for forty-five minutes!"

Fortunately, things went more smoothly with *Close Encounters* than with *Jaws*. And when it opened in November 1977, it was a huge hit. Within six months, it had earned more than $145 million! First *Jaws* was a big hit; now *Close Encounters* was, too. With two blockbuster movies to his name, it seemed as though Steven Spielberg could do no wrong.

But *Close Encounters of the Third Kind* was not the biggest hit of 1977. That honor went to *Star Wars*. The space adventure was made by Steven's friend George Lucas. It opened on Memorial Day weekend. And by the end of the summer, it had broken all box-office records—including the ones set by *Jaws*.

Early that summer, Steven had taken a break from working on *Close Encounters*. He went to Hawaii to relax. Who should be

Steven behind the camera again for the filming of Close Encounters.

staying close by but George Lucas, taking a vacation after the opening of *Star Wars*.

The two friends visited one another. George told Steven that he had been thinking of making a good old-fashioned adventure movie. Steven said that he had been thinking along the same lines. They talked over their ideas—and decided to work together. George

Lucas would produce the movie, and Steven Spielberg would direct it. They would hire Lawrence Kasdan, who wrote the script for *Star Wars*, to write the script for the adventure. But it was Lucas and Spielberg who planned the story.

Their hero would be a smart, tough, but friendly college professor. His adventures would take him around the world. He would get into nearly impossible situations, but always manage to find a way out.

His name: Indiana Jones.

Steven on location with Harrison Ford, star of the Indiana Jones movies.

While the scriptwriter was working on the Indiana Jones story, Steven began work on his next project. It was a comedy called *1941*. It starred John Belushi and other comedians from the hit TV show *Saturday Night Live*. Like *Jaws* and *Close Encounters*, *1941* had many special effects. It took months of hard work. But unlike Steven's first two major movies, it wasn't a big hit.

By the time *1941* had been released, the script for the first Indiana Jones movie was done. "I read it and wept," Steven later said. Did he cry because it was such a moving story? No, he said, he cried "because it looked like so much work!"

Still, Steven wanted to make the movie. And so *Raiders of the Lost Ark* was under way. And who would play Indiana Jones but actor Harrison Ford.

7

Raiders of the Lost Ark

A movie set is a very busy place—especially when an adventure movie is being shot. The sets for *Raiders of the Lost Ark* were no exception.

One scene in the movie was set in an ancient Egyptian tomb. Dozens of professional actors in costumes waited off camera. Workers adjusted lights and microphones. And as director, Steven Spielberg was in charge of it all.

But Steven was concerned. The scene he wanted to shoot called for forty-eight additional special actors. These actors had no experience. This would be their first—and last—movie. And right now, they didn't look too good.

The "actors" were forty-eight tarantula spiders.

The spiders were supposed to crawl over Indiana Jones and a villain he was fighting. They were supposed to be creepy and scary. But as Steven watched them in their pen, the spiders were listless. They just sat there. Lazy spiders were not scary enough.

Then Steven got a bright idea. He asked some workers to get electric fans and turn them on the spiders. A blast of cool air would wake them up, Steven thought. And he was right—too right!

"Nobody realized that the spiders could hop and climb," Steven later said, remembering what happened next. The deadly tarantulas, angry at being woken up, scrambled out of their pen. "A lot of them took off after the crew," Steven said. "People were running for their *lives*." Fortunately, no one was hurt that day. And for the most part, the filming of *Raiders of the Lost Ark* went smoothly.

Raiders is a rollicking adventure story set in the 1930s. In this movie, Indiana Jones stops the evil Nazi army from taking over the world with the Ark of the Covenant—a chest containing the ancient tablets on which the Ten Commandments were written. Indiana battles the bad guys all over the world— in the jungles of Central America, in the Himalayan mountains, in Egypt, and even on a remote desert island.

George Lucas and Steven Spielberg carefully mapped out the script for *Raiders*. It had sixty scenes, and each scene was two pages long. These scenes made up six "episodes" in the movie. Each episode was ten scenes long, and had a cliff-hanging climax. The thrills were as carefully planned as the ups and downs on a roller coaster.

To make the thrills come to life would take dozens of special effects, a huge cast, and many different exotic settings. Directing *Raiders* was a huge challenge.

But Steven was up to the challenge. *Raiders of the Lost Ark* stayed right on schedule. It cost $20 million to make. That is a lot of money, but it was actually *less* than George Lucas, the producer, had planned to spend on it.

How was Steven able to pull it off? With *Raiders of the Lost Ark*, Steven used what is called a storyboard. A storyboard is like a big comic strip. It shows every shot in a movie. A storyboard lets a director plan the whole story before a single camera rolls. After reading the script, Steven knew that filming the movie was going to be very complicated. So he planned it all down to the last detail. Every moment of the movie was "storyboarded" before shooting even began.

Of course, not every problem can be

solved on a storyboard. One scene called for Indiana Jones to have a fistfight on a runway as an airplane spins out of control around him. Before Steven could yell "Cut!" one of the airplane wheels rolled over Harrison Ford's leg. (Fortunately, it was so hot that the airplane's rubber wheels were soft, and Ford was not seriously hurt.)

And, of course, the cast included strange actors—like tarantulas. Another scene called for 6,000 snakes, including deadly cobras. (An ambulance stood by the set at all times during the snake scenes, its lights flashing, just in case.) The use of all these different animals made things very unpredictable.

One animal in particular gave Steven a very hard time. A main character in the movie is a cute monkey who turns out to be a Nazi spy. George Lucas visited the set the day Steven was filming the monkey's big scene. The monkey was supposed to salute like a Nazi soldier. But he just wouldn't do it.

Steven tried to bribe the monkey with grapes and bananas. Steven coached the monkey, making "Heil Hitler" salutes himself. But the monkey still would not salute. "I can't believe it," Lucas said, laughing at his friend. "He's smarter than you are!" Finally, after many frustrating attempts, Steven got the monkey to give his salute.

When *Raiders* came out, it was a big hit. Many critics thought it was Steven's best movie. And it was definitely good for Steven's career. After *1941* bombed, some people in Hollywood had wondered if Steven Spielberg was already washed up. They remembered the problems he had had filming *Jaws*. They were afraid he couldn't make a movie without going over budget. And pointing to *1941*—a comedy that wasn't very funny—they claimed Steven had no sense of humor.

But *Raiders of the Lost Ark* proved them wrong. With that movie, Steven made an

Steven directs Harrison Ford and Sean Connery in the third Indy movie, Indiana Jones and the Last Crusade.

exciting, entertaining movie. And he made it on time and under budget. Its success proved that Steven Spielberg was a great moviemaker. He could take on a huge, complicated project and make it into a hit.

But even though he had proved that he could handle it, Steven chose as his next project a movie that didn't have a huge cast or an exotic setting. In fact, it would be set in a typical American suburb. But it would be the biggest hit of all time.

Steven Spielberg with the "star" of the box-office smash E.T. The Extra-Terrestrial.

8

E.T.

A huge UFO, flashing colorful lights, rests in a forest. The area is bathed in warm moonlight. Strange creatures walk outside the UFO, gathering plants and animals. It is a scene of magic and wonder.

But the magic can't last. A group of men stalk the UFO. We don't see their faces, only their rushing feet as they crash through the forest. We see their flashlights darting through the night. The creatures hear the men approach and hurry back to their ship. The ship takes off with a blinding flash. The men watch, awestruck, as the ship disappears into the night sky. The UFO is gone.

But one scared, lonely creature is left behind. He is all alone in a strange and frightening world.

So begins *E.T. The Extra-Terrestrial*. From this simple story, Steven Spielberg created the most popular movie of all time. *E.T.* would be a favorite of kids all over the world. But believe it or not, Steven didn't always plan to make *E.T.* as a movie for kids. In fact, it started out as a horror movie!

When he was making *Close Encounters*, Steven wrote a story called *Night Skies*. It was similar to the first movie Steven ever made, the horror story *Firelight*. *Night Skies* was about a family in a lonely farmhouse. A UFO lands nearby. The aliens surround the house and terrify the family. All in all, it was a very spooky story.

Steven was too busy to work on *Night Skies*. So he hired a writer named John Sayles to write a screenplay based on the story. Sayles's screenplay made the story even scarier than Steven had planned. But Sayles also added a character that Steven had not thought of.

Although most of the aliens in the script were mean, there was one who was not. He was small and friendly. Sayles had put him in the script to give the story some humor. As Steven read the script, he got an idea for a different story. He liked the little alien and thought, "What if he got left behind? What if the little chap, the straggler, missed the bus home?"

After reading *Night Skies*, Steven went to work on *Raiders of the Lost Ark*. While making *Raiders*, he got to know a writer named Melissa Mathison. She was dating Harrison Ford at the time. (Later Ford and Mathison got married.) Mathison had written the screenplay for the hit movie *The Black Stallion*. Steven had enjoyed *The Black*

Stallion, and he told Mathison about the "little alien" idea that Sayles's character had inspired. She liked his idea and agreed to write the screenplay. And that's how *E.T.* was born.

When *Raiders* became a hit, Steven was free to do pretty much as he pleased. He began to work on *E.T.,* keeping the details top secret, though. When people asked what he was working on, Steven refused to tell. He wanted the story to be a surprise.

E.T., unlike *Raiders of the Lost Ark,* was not set in exotic locations. All of the action took place in the suburbs. So finding places to film it would be no problem. But the movie posed other big problems. For instance, who would be its "star"?

Steven didn't want E.T. to be a cute, cuddly alien. He wanted audiences to be a little bit put off by E.T.'s appearance. Steven thought E.T. should be "a creature that only a mother could love." But how could he show an ugly but lovable creature from outer space?

Steven hired an artist named Carlo Rambaldi to create E.T. As with Bruce, the shark in Jaws, there were three E.T. models made for the movie. They were made of latex, a flexible plastic, with electric motors under the skin that made each model move. One model was for full-body shots. It was bolted to the floor, and its body and face each could make thirty movements. The next one was for close-ups. It was loaded with electronic equipment and could make eighty-six different movements as it "acted." And one was a special suit that an actor wore, with radio-controlled arms. That model was used in scenes where E.T. was shown walking. In addition to the full-scale models, Rambaldi also made four E.T. "heads" that could show various emotions.

With his "star" made, Steven turned to his friend George Lucas for help with the

Steven directing an intense moment in E.T.

special effects. Lucas had started a business called Industrial Light and Magic. Its job is to create special effects for movies and TV shows. ILM, as it is known, is probably the best special-effects company in the world. Working with Steven, the artists at ILM created the models that would be used to show E.T.'s spaceship. They also masterminded the "magic" that let E.T. and his friend, Elliot, soar through the sky on a bicycle.

As soon as *E.T.* opened in June 1982, it

was a hit. People flocked to the theaters. Kids went to see it over and over again. Today, *E.T.* still stands as the greatest money-maker in entertainment history. The movie itself has made more money than any other—over $400 million. And more than $1 *billion* worth of *E.T.* "merchandise"—such as lunchboxes, T-shirts, and toys—has been sold! There is even an E.T. ride at the Universal Studios theme park.

What was the key to the movie's success?

Steven with Drew Barrymore, one
of the young stars of E.T.

Was it the awesome special effects? The funny and moving story? The great performances by Henry Thomas as Elliot and Drew Barrymore as his little sister, Gertie? All of those things played a part in the success of *E.T.* Still, many adults can't understand how such a simple "kiddie" movie could be such a huge hit.

But Steven Spielberg understands. The story is basically simple. Elliot tries to save E.T. from adult scientists who want to study him. That story is close to Steven's heart. "I always thought of the adult world as tall people who cast giant shadows," Steven said when *E.T.* came out. "People don't think like kids. They might understand E.T. scientifically. But they'd never understand that he had a heart."

But kids understand E.T. They know that underneath his ugly appearance, E.T. has a loving heart. They understand that, and they love him for it.

9

Busy Years

Think of the movies of the past dozen years or so. There have been many great movies for kids: *E.T.*, *Hook*, the three *Back to the Future* movies, the Indiana Jones trilogy, *Who Framed Roger Rabbit?*, *An American Tail*, *Fievel Goes West*, *The Land Before Time*, the *Gremlins* stories, *Young Sherlock Holmes*, *The Goonies*, and, most recently, *Jurassic Park*.

Believe it or not, Steven Spielberg worked on *all* of these movies.

Making movies is a risky business. It costs a lot of money to film a movie and to advertise it. A bad movie can lose millions of dollars. Even the best directors can have trouble raising money for a movie. But not Steven Spielberg. After *E.T.*, if Steven wanted to make a movie, it got made.

By the mid-1980s, Steven was working hard at being a producer as well as a director. A director controls how a movie is filmed—putting actors, lighting, sets, and special effects together. But producers are in charge of the whole process. They find the scripts, raise money, and hire directors and actors. (George Lucas produced *Raiders of the Lost Ark*, for example.)

In 1982, the same year *E.T.* was made, Steven had his first hit as a producer—a movie called *Poltergeist*. A ghost story about a haunted house, *Poltergeist* was as scary as *E.T.* was nice. "*Poltergeist* is the darker side of my nature," Steven said. "It's me when I was scaring my younger sisters half to death when we were growing up."

Steven went on to make more horror movies. In 1983, he produced a movie based on the old TV show *The Twilight Zone*. There were four segments in *Twilight Zone— The Movie*. Steven himself directed one of them. Unfortunately, *Twilight Zone* was struck by tragedy. A helicopter crashed during filming. Three actors—including two children—were killed. Steven Spielberg had nothing to do with the accident, but he still considers the event the low point in his career.

In 1984 and 1985, Steven produced two back-to-back hit movies. The first one was *Gremlins*, a wild horror/comedy. The title characters in *Gremlins* were mean and violent little creatures—kind of like E.T. gone bad. And kids loved them. Although some critics thought the movie was too violent and crude, it was a big hit. The next year, Steven had perhaps his biggest success as a producer.

Steven with Back to the Future
creator Robert Zemeckis.

Steven had had only one flop in his entire career as a filmmaker—the unfunny comedy *1941*. But he stayed loyal to the two men who wrote the movie, Bob Gale and Robert Zemeckis. Steven produced two more movies for them in the early 1980s. Neither one of them was a success. But in the mid-1980s, they showed Steven their newest script. It was a science fiction comedy about a teenager named Marty McFly who travels back in time and meets his parents when they were teenagers. It was called *Back to the Future*. Steven agreed to produce it.

Back to the Future turned out to be a big hit. Audiences and critics gave the movie rave reviews. It made Michael J. Fox into a movie star. And it proved that Steven was right to have faith in his friends and their talents.

Besides making popular movies, Steven returned to television. In the 1980s he produced a TV series called *Amazing Stories*. Like *The Twilight Zone* and *Night Gallery*, every episode of *Amazing Stories* told a different story. Steven never forgot how his career was helped by his work on *Night Gallery*. He hired talented young directors to make the episodes of *Amazing Stories*. Many directors working in Hollywood today got their first big break from Steven Spielberg.

*Steven in a promotional shot for his
television series* Amazing Stories.

Steven also helped to revive the art of animation. The period of the 1940s and 1950s
is sometimes called "the Golden Age of Animation." Warner Brothers made classic Bugs

Bunny cartoons back then. The Disney Studios were making *Fantasia* and other great animated movies. Steven and millions of other kids grew up watching those cartoons.

Then, in the 1960s and 1970s, theaters stopped showing cartoons. They were shown only on Saturday-morning TV. Most new cartoons were made quickly and cheaply. No one thought modern movie audiences would be interested in them.

But Steven remembered how much he had loved Bugs Bunny, Mickey Mouse, and all

Steven on location for an episode of Amazing Stories.

the rest of the great cartoon characters. He decided to bring cartoons back to the big screen. In 1988, he teamed up with Robert Zemeckis, the director of *Back to the Future*. Working with the Disney Studios, they developed *Who Framed Roger Rabbit?*, a movie that combined live actors with cartoon characters in a fast-moving comedy. The movie was a big hit. It proved that people of all ages still wanted to see cartoons.

Steven also produced a series of cartoon movies for younger kids. The first one was called *An American Tail*. It told the story of immigrant mice coming to America from Russia in the early 1900s. The hero of the movie is a six-year-old mouse named Fievel. Fievel was named after Steven's grandfather, who had come from Russia himself when he was a young boy.

Kids loved *An American Tail*. So together with the director, Don Bluth, Steven came up with another animated movie—*The Land*

Before Time. And working with directors Phil Nebbelink and Simon Wells, Steven produced a sequel to *An American Tail* called *Fievel Goes West*.

Although he was very busy producing movies, Steven did not give up directing. In 1984, Steven and George Lucas made a sequel to *Raiders of the Lost Ark*. The movie was called *Indiana Jones and the Temple of Doom*. Although it was a hit, the movie was controversial. After *E.T.*, many people thought of Steven as a director of kids' movies. They took their young children to see *Temple of Doom*. They expected to see a fun, but mild, adventure story.

They were very surprised. *Indiana Jones and the Temple of Doom* told a dark, sinister story. Although Indiana triumphs in the end, the movie is very violent. It shows torture, with kids chained and working as slaves in a mine pit. It's safe to say that *Indiana Jones and the Temple of Doom* was the cause of many, many nightmares. Quite a few parents felt that Steven had betrayed them.

Steven did not apologize for making the movie. He said that he and George Lucas had wanted to pit Indiana against the worst possible foes. "In this movie, our villains deal in black magic, torture, and slavery," he said. "So they're *really* bad."

Still, Steven understood why parents were upset. He felt that there should be a way to warn parents when they should not take little kids to a movie.

At that time, movies were rated G, PG, or R. "G," which stood for General Admission, meant that anyone could go in. "PG," or Parental Guidance, warned parents that the movie might not be right for kids. Kids couldn't get into Restricted, "R," movies unless an adult took them.

Some movies—like *Temple of Doom*—were okay for older kids, but not younger ones. So Steven suggested that there be a new rating between PG and R. As a result, there are now PG-13 movies. Kids under the age of thirteen can't get into a PG-13 movie without a parent, but older kids can.

Why was Steven suddenly so sensitive to parents and their concerns? Maybe it was because he now had a son. Back in 1976, Steven had met an actress named Amy Irving. They had dated off and on for years. In 1985, they had a son named Max. Later that year, Steven and Amy got married.

Having a wife and child seemed to change

Steven with his first wife, Amy Irving.

Steven. His movies were now more serious. In the late 1980s, Steven directed *The Color Purple* and *Empire of the Sun*—two very powerful movies for adults. Except for the final Indiana Jones movie, *Indiana Jones and the Last Crusade*, Steven seemed to have given up directing movies for kids.

Steven and Whoopi Goldberg at a party in New York City after a screening of The Color Purple.

Steven with John Malkovich and Christian Bale
on the set of Empire of the Sun.

The late 1980s were not easy years for Steven. His TV show, *Amazing Stories*, was canceled. His marriage to Amy Irving ended in divorce. And his next movie, a romance called *Always*, was far from successful.

Again, people in Hollywood wondered if Steven's magic had run out.

10

From Neverland to Jurassic Park

"I made this movie for one reason," Steven Spielberg has said. "I thought my kids would like it."

Steven was talking about *Hook*—his first movie in the 1990s. After making a series of movies for adults, Steven had decided to make another picture for kids.

Throughout the 1980s, rumors of a "super-movie" had buzzed around Hollywood. The rumor had it that Steven Spielberg planned to make a movie based on the classic J. M. Barrie story *Peter Pan*. The story told about a boy who never grew up. The rumors said that rock superstar Michael Jackson would play Peter Pan in the movie. As it turned out, the rumors about Michael Jackson were not true. But it *was* true that Steven wanted to tell the story of Peter Pan. He wanted to do it in a fresh, new way. Steven wanted to tell *Peter Pan* in his own style.

Then, in the late 1980s, Steven saw a script called *Hook*. It tells about Peter Banning, a successful man who never has time to spend with his kids. To make up for it, Banning takes his family on a trip to London. There, his kids disappear. As he begins to search for his children, a memory returns to Banning. He remembers that many years ago he was known as Peter Pan. Peter realizes that his children must have been kidnapped by the evil Captain Hook, and that he will have to return to his old home, Neverland, to save them.

Hook certainly was a fresh look at a familiar kids' story. But it also had a more serious message. In the 1980s, many people were driven to make a lot of money. *Hook* reminded people that material success and money aren't as important as spending time with your children.

Steven got three of Hollywood's biggest stars—Robin Williams, Dustin Hoffman, and Julia Roberts—to star in *Hook*. And the producers spent $60 million to create the fantasy. All of these things added up to make *Hook* a box-office success.

Steven worked very hard on *Hook*. But he still found the energy to begin work on his next movie. At about the same time that Steven began filming *Hook,* he heard about a new book about to be published. The author was a man named Michael Crichton. Steven had worked with Crichton before on a script called *Emergency Room*. Unfortunately, the movie had never been produced. Steven

*Steven and Robin Williams at a screening
of* Hook *in Los Angeles.*

didn't know much about Crichton's new
book, but he had heard it was about
dinosaurs.

Steven called Crichton on the phone. "I
said, 'You know, I've had a fascination with
dinosaurs all my life,'" Steven recalls. He

asked to see a copy of the manuscript. It was called *Jurassic Park*. As soon as he read the novel, Steven knew he wanted to make the movie.

But Steven wasn't alone. Many major studios fought for the movie rights to *Jurassic Park*. Warner Brothers wanted Tim Burton—maker of the Batman movies and *Edward Scissorhands*—to direct. Tristar wanted the story for director Richard Donner, who had done the Superman movies. But in the end, Crichton decided that it would be Steven Spielberg who would turn his story into a movie. It was not a hard choice to make, Crichton said. "Steven is...the most experienced and most successful director of these kinds of movies." As it turned out, Crichton made a good decision.

There are three main phases of making a movie. The planning stage is called pre-production. This is when the script is written and polished and when the sets and the special effects are designed. Then there is the production stage. This is when the movie is actually filmed. Finally, in post-production, the film is edited. Editors take all of the pieces of film and put them together into the final story you see in the theater. That's also when special-effects artists add their magic to a film.

In 1991, Steven went into production with *Hook*. Meanwhile, as the cameras rolled on that huge project, he was in pre-production on another film—*Jurassic Park*. He worked with Crichton on the screenplay. He supervised designers, who planned the elaborate sets for the movie. And he also worked with special-effects experts to plan the dinosaurs.

Most directors focus all of their time and energy on one project at a time. But not Steven Spielberg. Steven was working on *two* huge movies at the same time. And he had the skills to make them both successful.

"Steven was amazing to work with," Crichton says.

Hook came out at Christmastime in 1991, to mixed reviews. Some critics didn't like it. But many others thought it was an interesting new version of an old story. More important, though, the audiences liked it. *Hook* was a hit at the box office.

Most important of all, it was a success in Steven's eyes. He wanted to show people that his "kid" movies weren't just for little kids. They were made for the "kid" in everybody—even adults. Steven used Peter Pan to stand for the child in everyone. Through a child's eyes, "Neverland is not a cartoon world," Steven said, "it is a real place." And *Hook* helped people to remember that.

Now that *Hook* had been completed, Steven was able to turn all of his attention to *Jurassic Park*.

II
Jurassic Park

Dr. Jack Horner knows his dinosaurs. He is a paleontologist, a scientist who studies fossils. Horner has dug up dinosaur fossils all over the world. He is an expert on the extinct animals.

In the fall of 1992, Horner was visiting the set of Steven Spielberg's new movie as a consultant. Suddenly he came face to face with one of the stars. "I jumped about ten feet backward!" Horner later said. He had looked into the eyes of a real-live Tyrannosaurus rex!

Actually, the T-rex wasn't alive. It was a

model made for the movie *Jurassic Park*. Steven had worked with the special-effects artists to make the dinosaurs as real-looking as possible. "It was the closest I've ever been to a live dinosaur," Horner said. At forty feet long and twenty-five feet tall, and weighing nine tons, the model was certainly life-size!

Steven had hired Horner to give him advice as he made *Jurassic Park*. Why did he bother to enlist the help of one of the world's leading experts on dinosaurs? After all, *Jurassic Park* was only a movie. But Steven was determined to make it one of a kind. He wanted to be sure that the dinosaurs and the scenery were as accurate as possible. "I never wanted to do a dinosaur movie better than anyone else's," he has said. "But I did want my movie to be the most realistic of them all."

Jurassic Park is a fantasy, but it is based on the real science of genetic engineering. That is the science that allows people to clone—or make exact copies of—life forms. Today, scientists can make exact copies of animals like frogs using their DNA. Could they make copies of other animals—like dinosaurs—if only they had the material?

That is the basic idea of *Jurassic Park*. In the movie, scientists clone dinosaurs. They are to be the main "attractions" at a theme park on a remote tropical island. John Hammond, the man who owns the park, invites some scientists to inspect it before it opens. He also invites his two young grandchildren along to enjoy the park. In one terrible night, the dinosaurs rage out of control. Hammond, the scientists, and the children barely manage to escape—leaving the dinosaurs behind to rule the island.

It is an exciting story. But in order for it to be a good movie, the audience would have to believe that the dinosaurs were real. *That's* why Steven worked so hard on the special effects for *Jurassic Park*.

Why is Steven Spielberg such a perfection-ist when it comes to the effects in his movies? "My whole thing about special effects stems from being in school and hearing the word 'fakey,'" Steven told a reporter. "You know, you go back to class on Monday after every-one's seen a movie over the weekend. 'How'd you like the film?' '*Ah*. It was kinda *fakey*. Those weren't dinosaurs. They were big lizards with things glued on their backs.'"

No one can call the dinosaurs in *Jurassic Park* "fakey." "Steven made sure we showed them as animals, not monsters," said one of the special-effects artists who worked on the movie.

Steven used many different methods to bring the dinosaurs in *Jurassic Park* to life. In some scenes, model dinosaurs were used, just as in *Jaws* and *E.T.* They were made of foam rubber, were built to life size, and were run by motors hidden inside. The terrible T-rex that attacks the Land Rover truck, for instance, was the same life-size model that had frightened and impressed Dr. Jack Horner.

"Acting with these dinosaurs was wonderful," says Laura Dern, who played Dr. Ellie Sattler in the movie. In one scene, Dr. Sattler finds a sick triceratops—played by a full-scale model. "She was so beautiful and real," Dern says, remembering the model. "I was truly moved, as I am in the scene, just by being with her."

In another scene, the model dinosaurs were not quite as "beautiful." One high point in the movie is the kitchen scene. Lex and Tim, Hammond's grandkids, are stalked in a kitchen by a pair of killer velociraptors—vicious, birdlike dinosaurs. It was hard enough to show a tyrannosaurus attacking a truck on a dark, rainy night or to present a sick triceratops that just lay still. But to show a pair of eight-foot nimble dinosaurs stalking two kids through a kitchen was even harder.

But Steven and his special-effects artists had the skills to handle it. They used a number of methods to show the raptors. They built two puppets that were used for close-up "beauty shots." To show the walking raptors, the designers made a pair of raptor suits. Actors wore them and moved around the set. But how did the raptors swish their tails or tap their toes impatiently? The suits were hooked by cables to special-effects operators, who sat off camera. The cables linked up to motors inside the suits. Those motors made the motions that made the raptors come to life.

"On the set, it was actually more hilarious than frightening," says Steven. "Just under the kids, there would be three operators with remote controls, another six operators underneath the cameras, and twelve operators hiding in the cabinets. The actors were literally stepping over technicians to go through the actions of the scene." But on screen, you can see only the raptors and the kids—and it is *very* scary.

Another method Steven used to show dinosaurs was even more amazing. One scene called for a stampede of a herd of frightened gallimimuses. Another called for full-body shots of a huge brachiosaur. And for the climax of the movie, Steven wanted to show a fight between the T-rex and a number of raptors.

How could models be made for all of those different scenes? They weren't. Those dinosaurs were done with computer animation!

Take the scene where Dr. Grant and the two kids are almost run over by the galloping gallimimuses. Steven filmed the actors as they played the scene. They stood in awe and wonder as they stared at...nothing. The actors were looking at empty space, pretending that they were looking at the running dinosaurs. Then they ducked down behind a log, just as the dinosaurs were supposed to gallop over their heads. Special-effects artists had rigged up the log. Bark and chips of wood flew off it, as though the dinosaurs were running over it. But there was actually nothing there.

Months later, artists at Industrial Light and Magic looked at the film. They used computers to generate the dinosaurs that were seen on the screen. This was the first time that anyone had ever done anything like this. Until then, computer animation had been used only to make background scenes in movies like *Beauty and the Beast*. The liquid-metal robot in *Terminator 2* was also made with computers. But no one had ever before tried to use computers to show full-scale living animals. The results were astounding—even to Steven Spielberg.

"I hadn't been very aware of the technology until *Terminator 2* came out," Steven admits. "I thought it was possible that *someday* they might be able to create three-dimensional, live-action characters. But I didn't think it would happen this soon."

As if planning the shots, making the models, and working with computer artists was not hard enough, Steven had one more headache to deal with—Mother Nature. Many of the outdoor scenes in *Jurassic Park* were filmed on Kauai, one of the islands of Hawaii. On Friday, September 11, 1992, the movie crew had come to its last day of filming there. But it would be days until they could actually leave the island. On that day, Hurricane Iniki roared across the island!

Iniki was the worst storm to hit Hawaii in this century. It had winds of up to 180 miles an hour. Torrential rain lashed the island. The storm was so bad that it ripped the roof off the hotel where Steven and his crew were staying. "Iniki went through Kauai like the Big Bad Wolf at the house made of straw," Steven remembers. "Every single structure was in shambles. Roofs and walls were torn away. It was the worst devastation I had ever personally witnessed."

Fortunately, Steven and his crew had stayed right on schedule as they shot the movie. Their sets were destroyed by the storm, but they had finished using them. What's more, the crew was able to help out after the disaster. They helped to clear the roads around the hotel. They used the electrical generators from the movie sets to bring power back to the hotel. And Steven worked with the National Guard to aid others. He rented jet planes to fly to Kauai and take his crew back to California. Steven had the jets bring doctors, nurses, and medicine to help the injured people of Kauai.

All in all, filming *Jurassic Park* took an amazing amount of effort. But thanks to careful planning and hard work, Steven pulled it off without a hitch.

The results were spectacular. Critics

Steven with his wife, Kate Capshaw, at the premiere of Jurassic Park *in Los Angeles.*

hailed *Jurassic Park* as a historical landmark in moviemaking. People flocked to see the story, and they left believing that dinosaurs really did walk the earth once again. And, as before, a Steven Spielberg movie set box-office records.

Most important, though, Steven managed to please his toughest critics—kids.

"After 'Mommy,' 'Daddy,' 'yes,' and 'no,' often a child's fifth word is 'stegosaurus,'" Steven says. "Kids are completely dino-savvy at a very young age. I don't mind a letter from a seventy-year-old...carping about some little detail. But I don't want kids calling up and complaining that it wasn't real enough."

Thanks to Steven and the special-effects geniuses he hired, no one could complain about the dinosaurs of *Jurassic Park*.

12

Still Hungry

Today, you can visit Universal Studios in Hollywood, California. It is the same place where a young man named Steven Spielberg sneaked in to watch directors more than twenty years ago.

At the back of the studio lot is a beautiful mansion. It has a game room filled with pin-ball machines and video games. There is also a candy counter, a kitchen stocked with ice cream and popcorn, and a movie theater.

Is this mansion a playground? Is it a kids' dream-house come true? Not quite. It is the offices of Amblin Entertainment, Steven Spielberg's production company.

At any given time, there are about fifty movies or TV shows in progress at Amblin. Steven Spielberg keeps very busy. He produces the TV cartoon *Tiny Toon Adventures*. He also produced the violent thriller *Cape Fear*. And he works on just about every kind of show there is in between.

Steven is one of the most successful people in Hollywood history. The movies he has made have earned more than $4 billion. He is one of the richest men in show business. But he is also very generous. Steven has donated money to many different charities, ranging from ballet companies to dinosaur museums.

Steven also has a happy home life. He is now married to Kate Capshaw, who starred in *Indiana Jones and the Temple of Doom*. And he has five children. Three are his own birth children—two sons, Max and Sawyer,

Steven and Kate, again.

and a daughter, Sasha. Steven also has adopted Thea, an African-American girl Kate Capshaw had adopted before they were married, and Jessica, Capshaw's teenaged daughter. Steven lives with his family in a mansion overlooking Hollywood.

Even though he has a happy family life,

*Steven receiving the Golden Globe Award
for* Schindler's List.

Steven is one of the hardest-working people
you would ever want to meet. No sooner had
he finished *Jurassic Park* than he flew to
Europe to start his next movie—*Schindler's
List*.

Many people see Steven as the king of lighthearted entertainment. Even a scary movie like *Jurassic Park* is first and foremost fun. *Schindler's List* was a huge change for Steven. It is not a movie for kids. It is an adult drama that deals with one of the most serious topics in history.

The movie is based on an award-winning book by Thomas Keneally. It is a true story set in Poland during World War II. Nazi Germany had set up death camps in Poland and other countries. Their goal was to wipe out the Jewish population in Europe. More than

Steven posing with Schindler's List *stars Ben Kingsley and Ralph Fiennes.*

six million Jews were killed in those camps. This terrible period is called the Holocaust.

Schindler's List tells about a man named Oskar Schindler who used his contacts with the Nazi government to save thousands of Jewish people from the death camps. "Schindler's list" held the names of the people he managed to save.

Why did Steven choose to make *Schindler's List*? Steven is Jewish, and was made aware of the Holocaust as a young boy. His parents told him about it, and how he lost uncles and cousins to the death camps. "When I was very young, I remember my mother telling me about a friend of hers in Germany, a pianist," Steven has told a reporter. "She played a symphony that wasn't permitted, and the Germans came up on stage and broke every finger in her hands." *Schindler's List* was Steven's way of reminding the world of the terrible cruelty the Nazis showed to other people.

Steven attending the London premiere of Schindler's List.

The movie was a terrific success. Many critics say *Schindler's List* is one of the best—and most important—movies ever made.

Perhaps the most important "critics" are the people who were on Schindler's list. Many of them are still alive, thanks to Oskar

Schindler. Now the whole world knows their heartbreaking story—thanks to Steven Spielberg. "Spielberg just went into our hearts," one of them has said. "He saw what happened, he put it on the screen, and we love him for it."

What drives Steven Spielberg? Why does he always seek new challenges?

Perhaps it's because he still isn't satisfied with his work. Critics and audiences love Steven's movies. But in his opinion, he still hasn't made the perfect movie. Even though he is such a huge success, Steven says that he is "still hungry."

Still hungry? Steven Spielberg, the most powerful man in Hollywood? It's true. But Steven is not hungry for success. He's had more than his share of that. What is he hungry for?

It could be that he's hungry for the enchantment that movies can bring. More

Steven waving good-bye...

than anything else, Steven Spielberg remembers what it's like to be a kid. And he knows how a kid feels, sitting in a theater, waiting for the magic to begin.

On March 21, 1994, *Schindler's List* received a total of seven Academy Awards. Steven Spielberg received the award for Best Director, and *Schindler's List* was voted Best Picture.

THOMAS CONKLIN is also the author of *Muhammad Ali: The Fight for Respect,* another biography for young readers. A children's book editor, he lives in Maplewood, New Jersey, with his wife and their two dogs, Spud and Chester.

Bullseye Biographies

Meet Hillary Rodham Clinton
Meet Jim Henson
Meet John F. Kennedy
Meet Martin Luther King, Jr.
Meet Shaquille O'Neal
Meet Steven Spielberg
Meet Oprah Winfrey